Photo: Raymond Ross Photography, New York City

ISBN 0-7935-8752-2

7777 W. BLUEMOUND RD. P.O. BOX 13819 MILWAUKEE, WI 53213

For all works contained herein:
Unauthorized copying, arranging, adapting, recording or public performance is an infringement of copyright.
Infringers are liable under the law.

Visit Hal Leonard Online at
www.halleonard.com

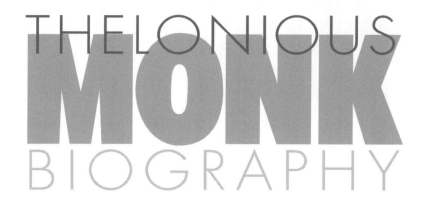

THELONIOUS MONK BIOGRAPHY

Thelonious Sphere Monk was born on October 10, 1917 in Rocky Mount, North Carolina. When he was four, his family moved to San Juan Hill, New York. His sister was the first in the family to take piano lessons, and Monk would learn by looking over her shoulder. Soon after, Monk was playing the piano in church and performing in the Apollo Theater's Amateur Contests. His playing style was developed early on, with his fingers flat and level on the keys, influenced by pianist Mary Lou Williams.

In the early 1940s, Monk was playing as a sideman in groups led by Kenny Clarke, Dizzy Gillespie and Charlie Parker. He became house pianist at Minton's Playhouse in Harlem, which eventually led to his first recording with the house quartet in 1941 while Charlie Christian was making a guest appearance. In 1944 Monk's signature tune "'Round Midnight" was recorded by Cootie Williams. Three years later, he made his first recordings under his own name for the Blue Note label. Between 1947 and 1952, Monk's output on the label would include recordings of the songs "Evidence," "Criss Cross," "Humph" and "Thelonious". These songs were the first indication of Monk's unique style of writing.

In 1951, Monk was arrested for narcotics and had his cabaret card taken from him, prohibiting him from working in New York nightclubs. He received a recording contract from Prestige Records in 1952, which lasted three years. During this period he recorded "Little Rootie Tootie", a song dedicated to his son, as well as his own eccentric version of "Smoke Gets in Your Eyes". Ultimately, the records didn't fare as well as other Prestige artists, such as Miles Davis and the Modern Jazz Quartet. Because of low sales, in 1955 Prestige Records sold his record contract to Riverside Records. This marked the beginning of a pivotal recording period in Monk's career. While at Riverside, Monk recorded such acclaimed albums as *Brilliant Corners*, *Thelonious Himself*, and *Thelonious Monk with John Coltrane*. While his unique style brought about controversy among jazz critics, these records established Monk as a composer and player.

By 1957, Thelonious Monk was allowed to play in nightclubs again. His first performance back was with a quartet at New York's Five Spot. This group featured John Coltrane, Wilbur Ware and Shadow Wilson, bringing even more attention to his music. He began to tour on a regular basis in both the U.S. and Europe. One concert in particular was a 1959 performance at New York's Town Hall, where a 10-piece orchestra performed Monk standards in expanded arrangements by Hall Overton. His rising popularity landed him on the cover of Time magazine in 1964, a rarity for a jazz musician.

In 1970, Monk disbanded his group. He went on to play with an all-star group in 1971-72 called the Giants of Jazz, which featured Dizzy Gillespie, Kai Winding, Sonny Stitt, Al McKibbon and Art Blakey. He also went on to make what would be some of his last recordings for the Black Lion label in 1971. It was after this that Monk suddenly decided to retire. Except for some festival appearances in 1975 and 1976, he spent his final years in seclusion at the home of Baroness Pannonica de Koenigswarter, a lifelong friend and patron. In 1982, Thelonious Monk died after suffering from a stroke at the age of 64.

CONTENTS

- 4   Blue Monk
- 12   Eronel
- 19   Evidence
- 28   Hackensack
- 36   Jackie-ing
- 43   Little Rootie Tootie
- 52   Monk's Point
- 64   North of the Sunset
- 68   Pannonica
- 57   'Round Midnight
- 90   Ruby, My Dear
- 74   Trinkle-Tinkle

Blue Monk
from *Thelonious Alone in San Francisco* (OJC-231)

By Thelonious Monk

Copyright © 1962 (Renewed 1990) by Thelonious Music Corp.
International Copyright Secured   All Rights Reserved

Eronel
from *Thelonious Monk – Piano Solo*(BMG-74321409362)
By Thelonious Monk

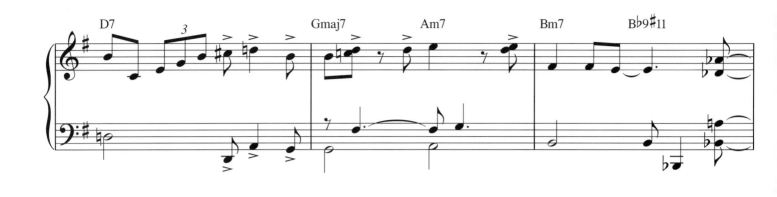
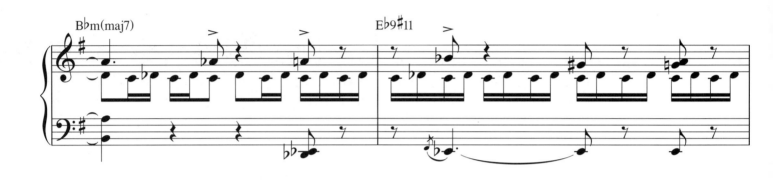
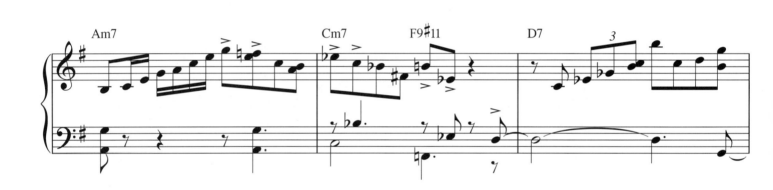
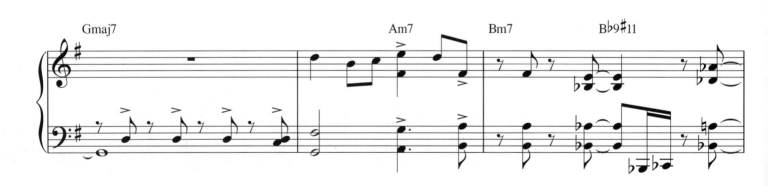

Evidence

from *Thelonious Monk – Piano Solo* (BMG-74321409362)

By Thelonious Monk

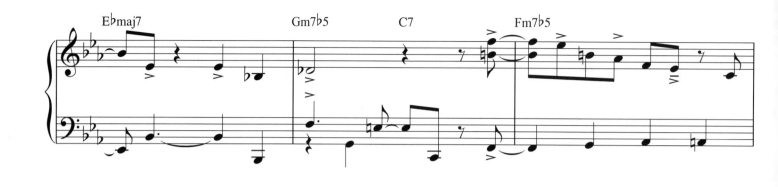

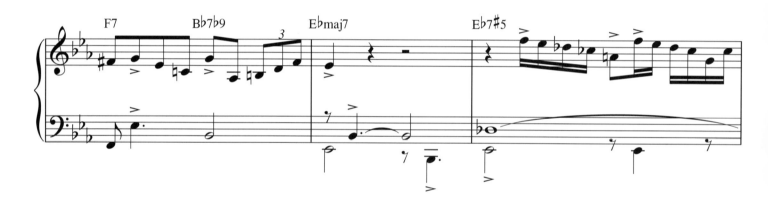
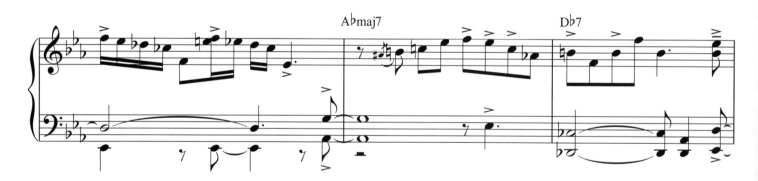
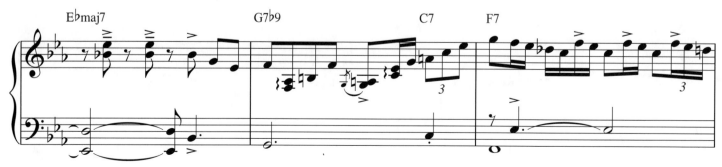

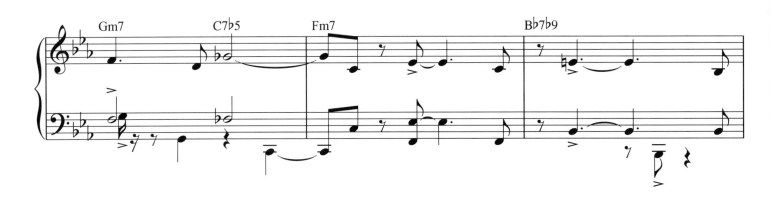

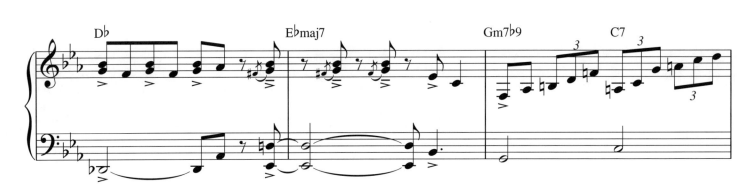

Hackensack

from *Thelonious Monk – Piano Solo* (BMG-74321409362)

By Thelonious Monk

Moderate Swing ♩ = 180

Copyright © 1978 by Thelonious Music Corp.
International Copyright Secured   All Rights Reserved

Jackie-ing
from *The London Collection Vol. 1* (1201 Music-9005-2)
By Thelonious Monk

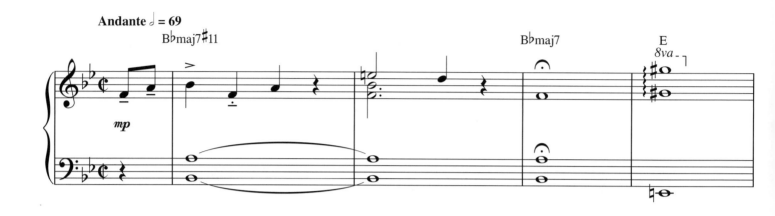
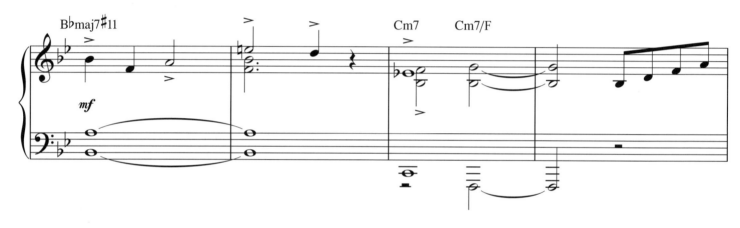
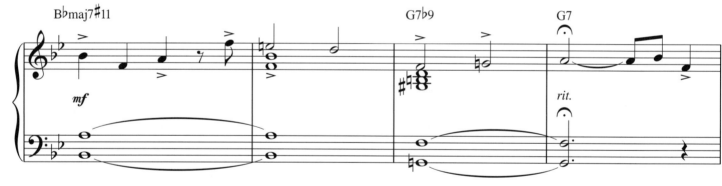
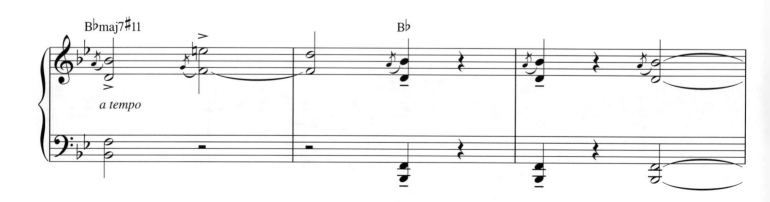

Copyright © 1978 by Thelonious Music Corp.
International Copyright Secured   All Rights Reserved

Little Rootie Tootie
from *The London Collection Vol. 1* (1201 Music-9005-2)

By Thelonious Monk

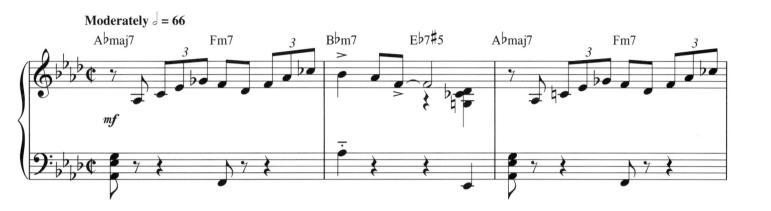

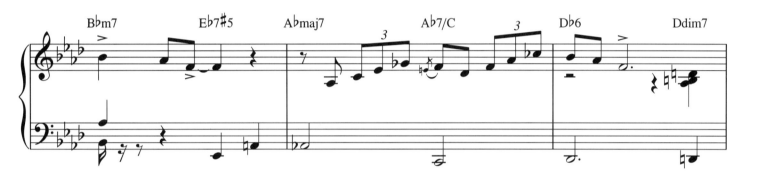

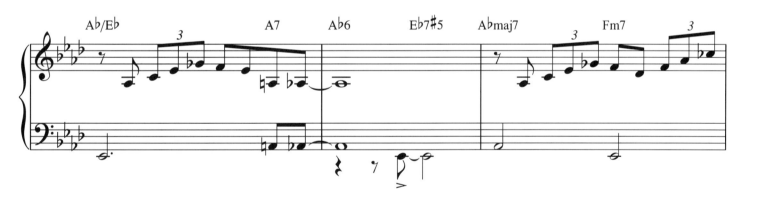

Copyright © 1978 by Thelonious Music Corp.
International Copyright Secured   All Rights Reserved

Monk's Point
from *Solo Monk* (Columbia Legacy-47854)

By Thelonious Monk

52

North of the Sunset
from *Solo Monk* (Columbia Legacy-47854)
By Thelonious Monk

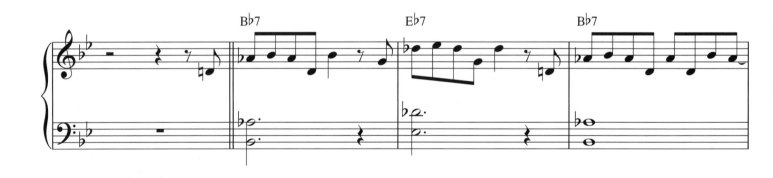
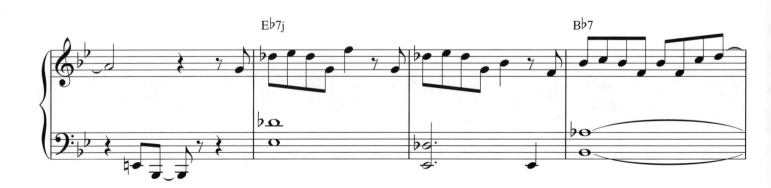

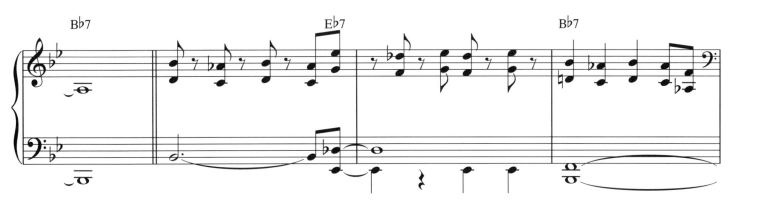
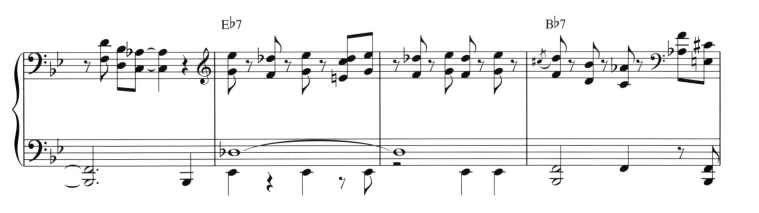

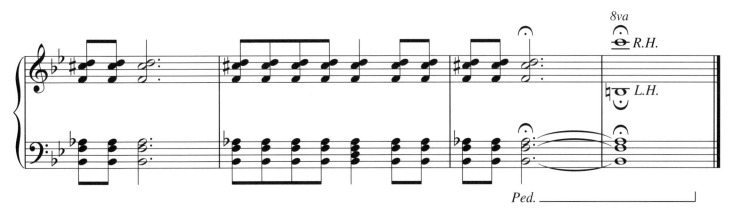

Pannonica
from *Thelonious Alone in San Francisco* (OJC-231)
By Thelonious Monk

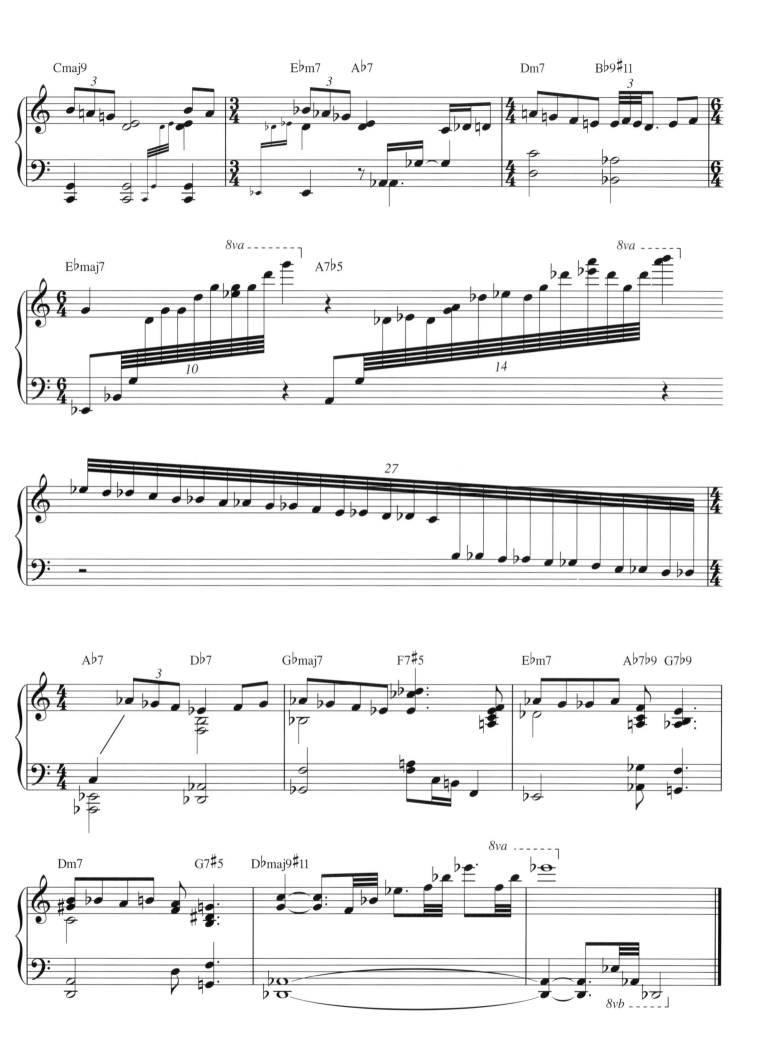

Trinkle-Tinkle
from *The London Collection Vol. 1* (1201 Music-9005-2)
By Thelonious Monk

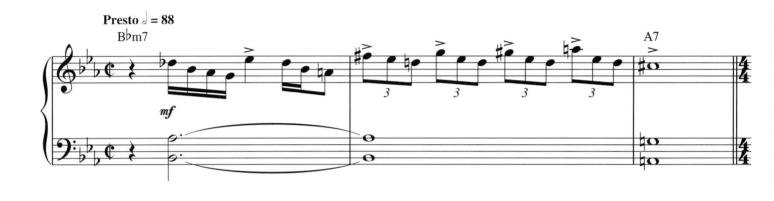
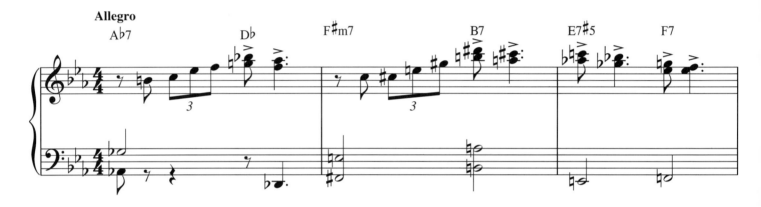

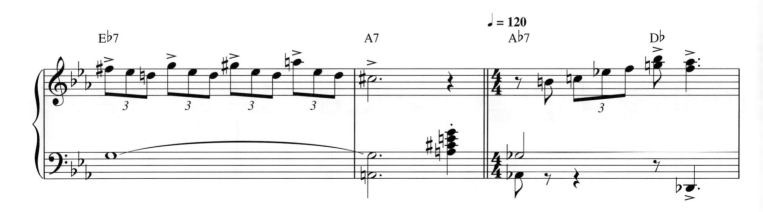

Copyright © 1962 (Renewed 1990) by Thelonious Music Corp.
International Copyright Secured All Rights Reserved

Ruby, My Dear
from *Solo Monk* (Columbia Legacy-47854)
By Thelonious Monk

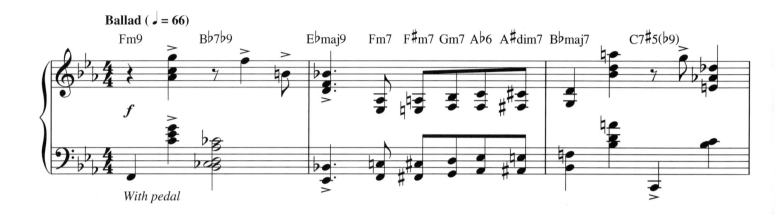
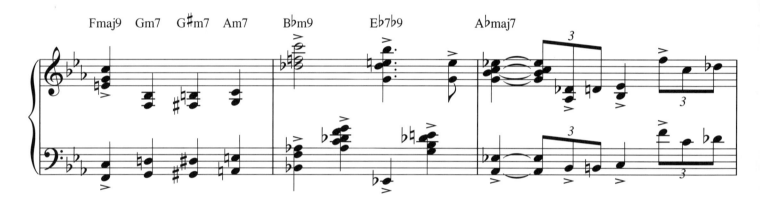
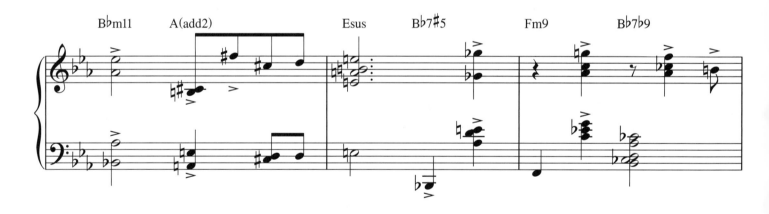